CONTENTS

KU-131-957

What is a street gang? 4

Are school gangs a problem? 6

Are gangs a new issue? 8

Why join a gang? 10

Can gangs keep you safe? 12

Their own choice to join? 14

Are girl gangs dangerous? 16

Does gang style matter? 18

Graffiti – tagger's art or gang warning? 20

Can gangs be a good force? 22

Are gangs glamorous? 24

Do drugs bring gangs riches? 26

Do gang members enjoy violence? 28

Do gangs only target rival gangs? 30

Are gang members victims or villains? 32

Does jailing gang members work? 34

Can gangs be stopped? 36

Should parents do more to help? 38

Is leaving a gang easy? 40

Conclusion 42

Timeline 44

Glossary 46

Resources 47

Index 48

WHAT IS A STREET GANG?

Some people call any group of young adults a gang. This book is about street gangs – groups linked by signs, symbols and clothing. Street gangs perform anti-social acts and crime.

Big in the USA

Gangs exist all over the world. There are an estimated 10,000 skinhead gang members in the Russian city of Moscow alone. The United States is believed to have more street gangs than any other country. According to Larry Clark, a police chief in the USA, the problem has grown recently:

❝ If you look over a period of time... the last 10 years, there's no question that there's not only been an increase in violence, but a drastic increase in the number of gang members and crimes associated with gang members. ❞

Three members of a street gang in Cali, Colombia. Cali is home to some 200 gangs, known as pandillas.

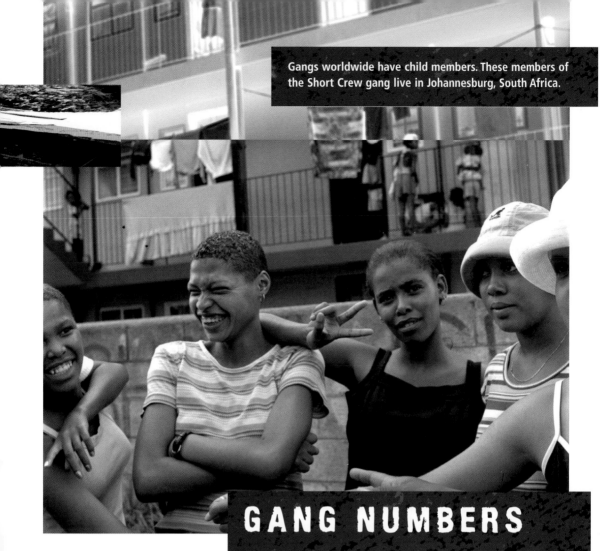

Gangs worldwide have child members. These members of the Short Crew gang live in Johannesburg, South Africa.

GANG NUMBERS

Global gangs

There are links between gangs in different countries. Central American gangs are known as maras. They have spread through Honduras, El Salvador and most of Central America as well as into the USA. Jose Marciago Molina, 20, was shot in Mexico by a mara gang who robbed him:

Country statistics on gangs and their members are rare. Detailed national statistics are only collected in the USA, where the problem is believed to be worst.

COUNTRY	USA	UK	NEW ZEALAND	CANADA
TOTAL POPULATION (2005)	296m	60m	4m	33m
GANG MEMBERS	731,000	20–30,000	4–11,000	7,100
GANG NUMBERS	21,500	unknown	70 plus	434

(Gang figures 2002–03)

❝ I left Honduras because I didn't want any problems with the maras, because you can't even go out on the street there. I started to run, and they shot me in the back. They took everything I had, even my shoes. I now walk on crutches because the bullet is lodged near my spine. ❞

ARE SCHOOL GANGS A PROBLEM?

Many children are in a gang at school. It makes them feel part of a group of mates. Are school gangs just a part of growing up? Or can they lead to problems such as bullying, violence and crime?

Just a bit of fun

Peter, 13, lives in Staines near London, UK. His gang of friends sometimes get accused of being troublemakers, but he maintains they have never done anything wrong:

" My gang started at school. We're just a group of friends, right, who hang out together and have a good time. My gang go the arcade and the park and just muck around, playing football and stuff. We have some secret hand signs we copied from movies and videos, which is cool. Aren't we better sticking together than being sad loners with no mates? "

This group of British school friends hang out together but do not form an organised gang.

Leading to problems

Some school gang members dare each other to perform small crimes such as shoplifting, which can lead to more serious crime. Stefan describes his school gang in Sydney, Australia:

❝ All I had to do to join was steal a CD from the market. But as our gang grew, the stuff they made new 'uns do got out of hand. Two boys were told to steal a girl's mobile phone from school. They did that. One kid, Greg, had to jack [steal] a car to get in with us. Then, the girl's brother, who was in another gang, challenged us to a fight. It got scary, one kid got knifed. I got out of it. It was too much. ❞

The parents of Katherine Bamber and an image of their daughter, who hung herself in 1992 after being bullied at school by an all-girl gang.

"Youths learn to take risks. For those involved in youth gangs, risk taking involves violence and the endangerment of themselves and others."
Valerie Wiener, *Winning the War Against Youth Gangs,* USA, 1999.

ARE GANGS A NEW ISSUE?

Gangs are often reported in the media as a modern issue. The number of teenage members of gangs has increased in many countries in the past 20 years. Have gangs existed for a long time?

Family influence

Some gangs have kept on going for 60 years or more through different generations of families. Eddie Banales runs religious programs in Pomona, California to help keep kids out of gangs. In the 1970s and early 1980s, he was a member of the Pomona 12th Street gang in the USA:

❝ It is a family thing... when your mom and dad and brothers and sisters and grandparents and great grandparents all were a part of the gang, it is all you know. It is almost as if you don't have much of a choice but to grow up into that gang lifestyle. ❞

A scene from the 1996 film, *Romeo and Juliet*, which updated the Shakespeare play and placed it in a gangland setting.

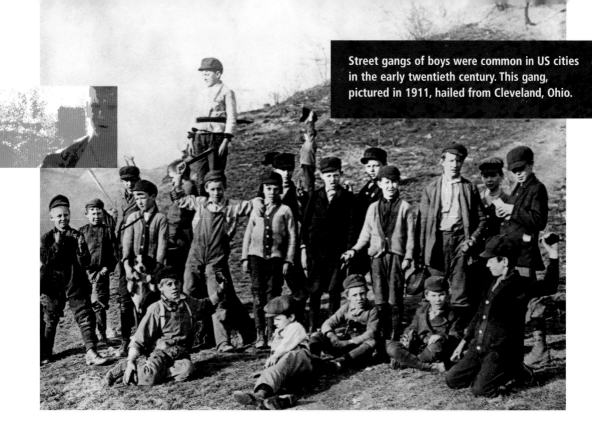

Street gangs of boys were common in US cities in the early twentieth century. This gang, pictured in 1911, hailed from Cleveland, Ohio.

Long, long ago

Gangs have existed for many centuries. The word 'thug', for example, comes from India: around 800 years ago, 'thugz' meant a gang of criminals. About 400 years ago, London was terrorised by gangs such as the Hectors, the Dead Boys and the Bugles, then later by the Mohawks:

 **In the early 1700s, it was the Mohawks who kept Londoners in a constant state of terror with their favourite pastime – Tipping the Lion. This meant smashing someone's nose with a huge piece of iron and gouging their eyes with thumbs. Few Londoners ventured out at night for fear of 'being mohawked'.** "

YOUTH GANGS

The number of US cities reporting youth gang problems rose from 270 in the 1970s to 2,547 in 1998.

NUMBER OF CITIES IN THE USA WITH GANGS

	1970S	1998
South	22	730
Midwest	32	717
North-east	41	341
West	175	759

WHY JOIN A GANG?

People join gangs for different reasons. Many join because their friends are already members or they want to belong and be supported by a close group. Do gangs really provide support, trust and friendship?

A kind of family

Many people in gangs join so that they can gain attention and feel part of a group. They may feel very close to the other members, who may support them through difficulties. Darren, a member of a teenage gang in Manchester, UK, says:

❝ I know my brothers will stand beside me whatever happens. If people come after me, they're not coming after just me. They're coming after the whole gang, because everyone looks after everyone else. ❞

Darren calls the other people in his gang his 'brothers'. Gang members often say that the gang has taken the place of their family.

New members of gangs often have to perform crimes such as shoplifting or car theft or endure a violent beating as part of the process of joining.

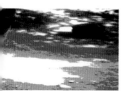

Beaten and betrayed

Many gangs have some sort of initiation act before joining. One of the most common is to be 'beaten in' to a gang. For Shank, a member of a New York gang, the beating he received made him think again about his so-called friends:

❝ They put you in a circle and everybody starts hitting you – your own friends. It hurts. It hurts your heart. It makes you feel bad, like you can't be totally friends, and it puts you in a spot where you can't even trust your own friends. Anybody in a gang or crew will tell you they don't trust nobody. ❞

A new member of the Mara Salvatrucha gang in El Salvador is beaten in for 30 seconds.

"Getting into a gang is easy. They just open a door for you. They say they are your friends, but when it comes down to it, they're there to hurt you and make you take money from those close to you."

Brian Contois, former leader of Manitoba Warriors gang in Canada, 2001.

CAN GANGS KEEP YOU SAFE?

Life in many cities is hard. Crime and violence threaten many young people, especially in poor areas. Gangs promise to look after their members. Can gangs keep members safe or do they put them in more danger?

Respect and survive

Coki is a member of New York gang Flushing's Top Society (FTS). He believes that being in a gang gives you respect in a tough neighbourhood and is the only way to survive:

❝ If you don't have respect on the street then you're gonna get picked on, always. If you're not gonna get robbed on the street then you're gonna get hit on the street, if not that, then someone is gonna do something to you, so you can't let that happen. ❞

Gang members cruise by the playground of the Horace Mann Junior High School in Los Angeles, USA.

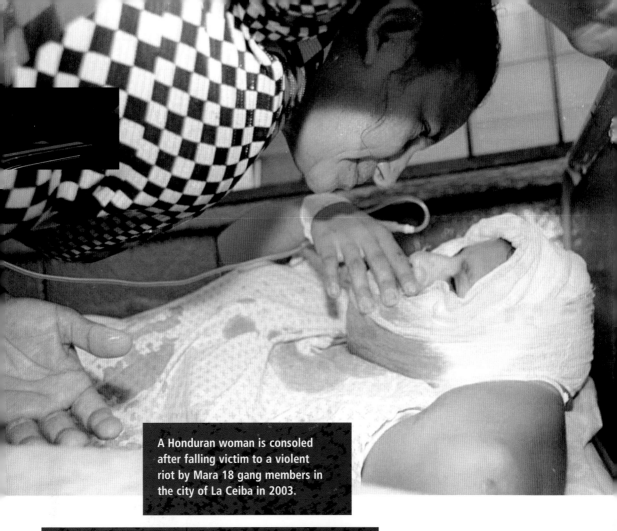

A Honduran woman is consoled after falling victim to a violent riot by Mara 18 gang members in the city of La Ceiba in 2003.

MURDER ONE

Fatalities through murder, Los Angeles, USA

YEAR	GANG MEMBERS	NON-MEMBERS
1990	97 per 1000	13 per 1000
1995	106 per 1000	17 per 1000
2000	122 per 1000	19 per 1000

In danger

Ramon is a former member of a Hispanic gang in Los Angeles, USA. Looking back, he feels that his gang actually put him in much more danger:

❝ I joined the gang because my brother was already in it. I was a little kid, but soon they had me doing all kinds of illegal stuff. I spent time in jail, missed my education and my arms are covered in gang tattoos. I sometimes think I was lucky to get out alive. ❞

"Gang culture is now inextricably linked with gun violence."
Steve Shropshire, UK expert on gangs and youth culture, 2002.

THEIR OWN CHOICE TO JOIN?

Gangs need members to thrive, and in very violent gangs, to replace those members who are seriously injured, killed or imprisoned. Do new gang members join of their own free will or are they forced or tricked into membership?

Threatened and harassed

Some gangs harass and threaten vulnerable young people into joining them. Gregorz felt forced into joining a gang in Krakow, Poland in this way:

“ Kochi helped me with a bully at school. I said I owed him but he said, 'no, you owe the brothers'. I was asked to look after a car – turned out, it was stolen. Kochi threatened to tell my family and the police if I didn't join his gang. If not, he said his gang might hurt my little sister. I had no choice. ”

A skinhead breaks into a car. Young people who have friends who are gang members are often lured into gang life.

Some films and music have made gangs look cool or glamorous. The 1988 movie, *Colors*, was criticised for using as extras real-life members of the Bloods and Crips gangs.

Getting in on the action

Gang members boast of their reputation, the excitement of being in a gang and the money and power they have earned. Many young wannabes are keen to get a slice of the action. Ranell, 23, joined the Mafia Insane Vice Lords gang in Chicago, USA when he was just 10:

❝ You see this guy and he's got a nice car, a nice setup.... You don't want nothin' else but what he's got. Gang leaders don't mind showing the young guys how they got the nice car. They'll say, 'Let me show you, you go out there and get rid of this [drug] and I'll give you a little something.' Little by little, they get into it. ❞

ARE GIRL GANGS DANGEROUS?

Many people think of boys as more violent than girls and assume that only boys are active gang members. But there are some mixed gangs. Girls also form their own all-girl gangs. Are these a problem?

Helping out the boys

Police gang investigator Sergeant Lou Perez says it may differ from city to city, but in San Francisco, female gangs and gang members are mainly on the sidelines, helping the male members:

❝ The boys basically are mostly violent. They commit the majority of violent crime, the homicides, the drive-by shootings, the robberies. The girl gangs act as their accessories [helpers]. They will help them to commit these crimes. They will hide weapons for them, they'll hide narcotics [drugs] for them.... ❞

Four members of the El Salvadorian gang, Gang 18, flash their signs for the number 18.

Violent girls

But in some places, all-girl gangs can be violent and commit crime. Tiny was a founder member of the Nasty Fly Ladies (NFL) all-female gang in New York, USA:

❝ See, we smaller girls, we go for your weak spot. Your face. Your throat. Your eyes, so we can blind you. I don't care if you have more weight on me. I'll still try to kill you because, you know, I have a bad temper.... It's like the anger will kill you! Today I had a fight with my boyfriend and I pulled a knife on him. He tried to grab it and I sliced his hand. It doesn't matter when you have anger. ❞

Girl gang members in Brooklyn, New York. The girl on the right is practising hiding a razor blade as a weapon inside her mouth.

GIRLS IN GANGS

According to the US National Youth Gang Survey (2002), an estimated 8% of gang members are female. Other studies have shown female gang membership to be as high as 38%.

"The role of girls in gangs is changing – they are younger, tougher, and are just as violent, sometimes more, than their male counterparts."
Chicago Crime Commission, 2002.

DOES GANG STYLE MATTER?

Gang members show their identity in many different ways. These include their clothing and tattoos and the slang they speak. They use special hand signals, called flashing. Does it matter to gang members if others copy them?

It's just fashion

Many symbols of American gangs are now part of fashion. Jake, 15, is not in a street gang but admires the fashions:

❝ I've always liked the colour red and I like the style of gang clothes so I call myself a Blood. It's not just me, loads of friends wear symbols and the number 13 [a symbol of famous Hispanic gangs such as MS-13]. ❞

Brandishing guns, members of the Crips in Compton, Los Angeles wear their traditional blue gang colours.

In recent years, traditional Maori face tattoos, called *ta moko*, have been adopted by many New Zealand gang members.

A dangerous game

For gang members, showing gang identity is deadly serious. Willy-D was in the Crips in Los Angeles in the late 1990s. He recalls how what you wore and the symbols you used could be a matter of life and death:

❝ We had a whole bunch of stuff to make it clear who we were and how you don't mess with us. We wore British Knights sneakers as the BK stood for Bloods Killer and man, your life depended on you wearing the colour blue in the right way. One of our new homies forgot to wear a blue bandana, our colour, and then stupidly didn't flash one of our set with the right signs when he was uptown. He got capped [shot] in the leg three times. He was lucky. Others have been killed. ❞

"Be aware of clothing, colours and symbols used by gangs in your area, and avoid them. If you *look* like a gang member or are *seen* with a gang member, other gangs may mistake you for a *real* gang member."

National Youth Violence Prevention Center, USA, 2005.

GRAFFITI - TAGGER'S ART OR GANG WARNING?

Graffiti is writing, symbols or pictures painted, scratched or written on to walls, signs and buildings. Most people don't like graffiti because it is vandalism and it makes them feel unsafe. Is vandalism a sign of gang action or just street art?

Just tagging

Taggers produce graffiti illegally for the thrill but are rarely a part of street gangs, although they may be asked to perform graffiti for gangs. Many taggers work together in crews. Javier is a teenage tagger in Nevada, USA who prefers to work alone:

❝ Graffiti is pure freedom. And in its rawest, purest form is [done] illegally on the street. Graffiti art is addictive. It is productive, fun and active. You're not sitting at home watching TV. It's an outlet. ❞

A German youth completes graffiti on a wall in Frankfurt. The cost of cleaning up graffiti is huge.

A teenager in Los Angeles, USA tags a building with his gang's signs.

"Gang members take the messages they read in graffiti seriously, and the longer graffiti is left up in a neighbourhood, the greater the risk that the threats will be acted upon."

Janene Rae, Director, Off the Wall (graffiti-reducing programme), USA, 2005.

Harmless fun?

Graffiti has several purposes according to Steven L. Sachs, a probation officer and author of *Street Gang Awareness* (1997):

❝ Graffiti serves as a warning and challenge to other gangs. Graffiti can also honour a fallen comrade (usually by showing a tombstone or writing 'RIP'), list the street names (nicknames) of gang members, and show opposition and disrespect for another gang. Gangs have been known to retaliate against individuals painting over their graffiti. ❞

Violence can occur if one gang crosses out the graffiti of another, or if a gang is disrespected using graffiti. Graffiti threats in the USA include crossing out or writing 187 (the police code number for homicide) next to a rival gang or gang member's name.

CAN GANGS BE A GOOD FORCE?

Gangs tend to operate in a clearly defined area known as their turf or hood, short for home neighbourhood. Some gang members say that they help to keep their neighbourhood safe.

Protecting the neighbourhood?

Many crimes are committed by criminals not in gangs. Hernandez, 16, is a member of the Gangster Disciples (GD) gang in Chicago, USA. He thinks that gangs can help a community by protecting it from crime:

" It's not all gangbanging and stuff like that. To me, GD could stand for Growth and Development.... It's like we're here to help out the neighbourhood. We're more into protecting than anything else. It's a pride thing, pride and loyalty to the neighbourhood where you live. "

Young Kurdish members of the Sioux gang in Berlin, Germany. Under threat from racist gangs, some immigrants band together for security.

> **"Unlike Robin Hood, their menacing influence on the community far outweighs their generosity to the community."**
> William O'Brien, Narcotics Prosecutions Bureau, Cook County, USA, 2002.

Russian officers arrest a young drug-dealing gang member in Kaluga. Many gangs commit crime.

Turning into a war zone

Dana lives in a poor neighbourhood in Manchester, UK. Infamous gangs in her area, such as the Longsight Crew and the Gooch, have made life worse not better:

❝ It was never paradise here but now it's a war zone thanks to the gangs. Some parts are no-go areas, there's graffiti everywhere and you're afraid to go out after dark – so you're a prisoner in your own home afternoons and evenings. The police don't know the half of it. You're too afraid to report crimes in case the gangs see the police at your door. Then, there'll be more trouble. A new children's playground was built but parents are too afraid to let kids play there in case the gangs try to recruit them or hurt them. ❞

ARE GANGS GLAMOROUS?

New gang members may feel a rush when a gang lets them in. Are they joining a glamorous outfit or are they simply at the bottom of the pile, with little chance of an exciting life?

King of the hood

Gang life is made to look glamorous in movies and videos for gangster rap music. For Aless-D in Melbourne, Australia, gang life really is like that:

" There's four of us who are OGs [original gangsters – the gang leaders], another 9 or 10 brothers who are hardcore and maybe 20 or 25 boys who do the work. We OGs get the respect and move anywhere in the city. I get all the girls I want, got money, got power. Just fear one day it will be taken from me. "

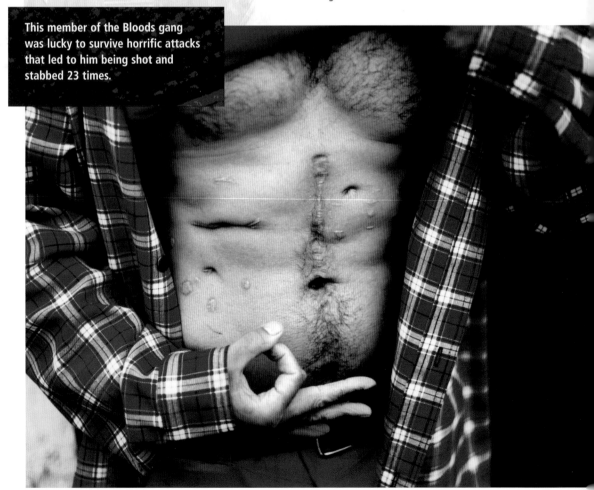

This member of the Bloods gang was lucky to survive horrific attacks that led to him being shot and stabbed 23 times.

A 13-year-old Colombian gang member, known as 'La Chinga', handles one of the guns he has used to kill five people.

A dull, dangerous existence

The reality of gang life is often not glamorous but dull or dangerous, as Alexei, a member of a gang in Moscow, Russia, discovered:

❝ Gang life seemed so exciting from the outside. You see the big money made by gangs in Russia on TV but the gang I joined were just street punks acting big. We'd spend our time trying to pick fights with others and getting beaten for not respecting our leaders enough. All the gang rules and signs, the stupid caring about who sprays what tags on a wall. It was boring and dull. Most of the time we just looked to get high, sniffing glue or *karat* (leather dye) and trying to steal to make money. ❞

"Gangs are glorified. Some join gangs for protection, but for most of them, they're looking for power, status and excitement."
Danya Perry, North Carolina Department of Juvenile Justice and Delinquency Prevention, 2003.

DO DRUGS BRING GANGS RICHES?

Many street gang members sell drugs on the street to make money. Do they become rich?

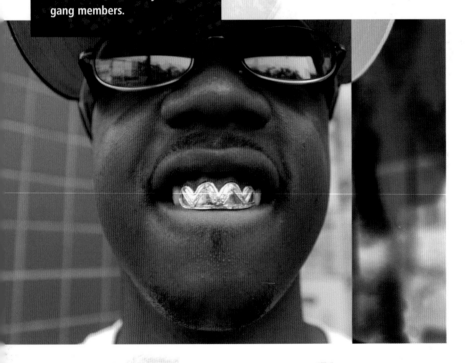

An American man displays removable gold and silver teeth caps. Similar displays of wealth are used by senior gang members.

Making money

Selling drugs on the street is dangerous but some teens in gangs see it as the only way to make money. Sticky, 16, is a shotta (a person who delivers drugs for drugs dealers) in Nottingham, UK:

> **A shotta is just like a paper boy making deliveries. To be a shotta you need a mobile phone, transport and then you go poaching, which is taking other's customers. A top shotta will be driving around, earning £1,400 a week but he doesn't touch the stuff. Others are selling it for him.**

"Most gang members make very little money being part of a gang. Getting your education is the key to making money, not joining a gang."
Michelle Arciaga, National Youth Gang Center, USA, 2001.

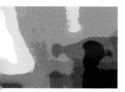

Drug addiction

Most illegal drugs are very addictive and bring misery to those who take them. Many gang members become hooked on the drugs their gang sells and become poor and desperate addicts. An El Salvadorian, Jaime, was a member of the Mara Salvatrucha gang, one of the most infamous gangs in Central America and the USA. Jaime became a drug addict and recalls:

" The worst thing was that my six-month-old son was malnourished because my girlfriend couldn't afford to buy him any milk... he'd just get the occasional fizzy drink because I was using all the money for drugs. "

SELLING DRUGS

According to the 1999 Youth Gang Survey:

● 46% of youth gang members in the USA were involved in drug sales.

● Gang members aged 15 were three to five times more likely to be selling drugs than non-gang members.

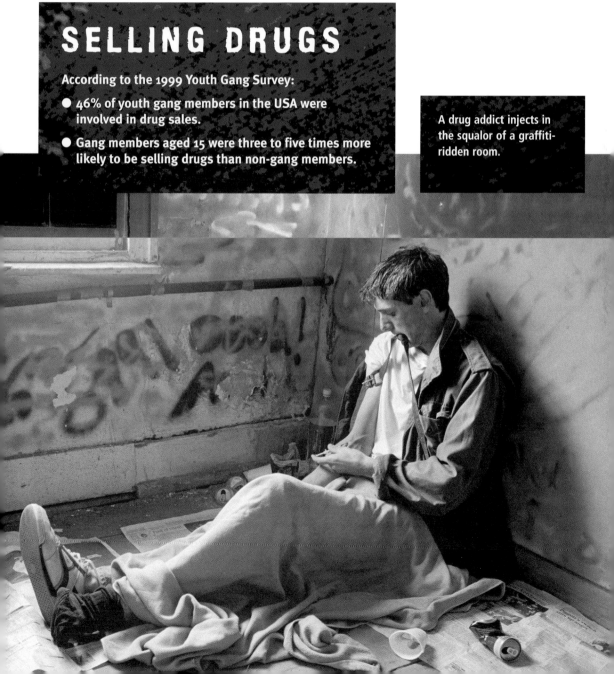

A drug addict injects in the squalor of a graffiti-ridden room.

DO GANG MEMBERS ENJOY VIOLENCE?

Gangs are responsible for much violent crime. Some members relish the violence and enjoy the added respect they gain from others in the gang. Others feel fearful of the violent world around them.

Smiles turning sour

Some gang members find the reality of gang violence shocks them. Didi remembers when his gang in Marseilles, France, fought a serious turf war with a rival gang:

" We were all laughing and joking as we walked up to them. They smiled as well. I had a chain with me. Others had knives. Then it started. I was stabbed in the arm. One of the pigs [rivals] pulled a gun and shot my friend, Jean. Blood was everywhere. Jean was screaming. I felt sick, couldn't fight. I ran. **"**

NUMBER OF UNDER-18 GANG KILLINGS, USA

1999	2000	2001	2002	2003
580	653	862	911	819

"A lot of times people don't want to kill one another but they have to, because there's so much pressure, and they got a gun."

Theophus Brooks, head of the Washington, DC Youth Gang Task Force, 2004.

Two London gangs clash in a reconstruction for a British television documentary.

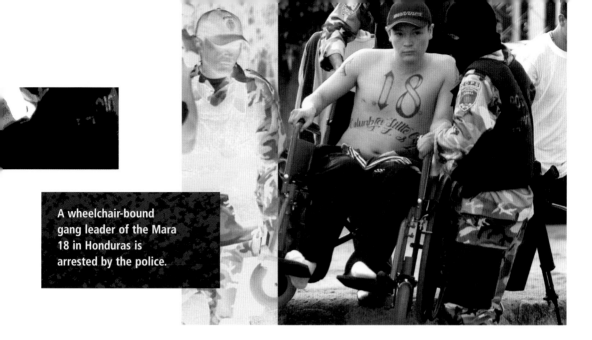

A wheelchair-bound gang leader of the Mara 18 in Honduras is arrested by the police.

Violence brings power

To some, like Bill, an ex-gang member from Canada, gangs enable them to use violence to feel powerful:

" I mean, if you see someone quivering at your feet, it makes you feel like: 'Yeah, I have power over this person. It's a head buzz.... Even though the guy might be six-foot-six [2m tall] and you're only five-foot-ten [1m 80cm], you've got four of your friends [so] this guy is scared of you. It makes you feel you're untouchable. "

DO GANGS ONLY TARGET RIVAL GANGS?

DAVID LEON HARRIS, JR.
Sept. 5, 1975 — Sept. 25, 1994
Why he had to die, I don't know
You and I both loved WY'NO
NHBDS is what he was
One of a kind and a true

Gangs spend much of their energy disrespecting rival gangs and retaliating violently when a rival gang challenges them. Do they only attack each other?

Turf wars

Turf wars are when gangs fight over territory and control of drugs sales. In the UK, some young gang members carry a bora – an air pistol altered to fire real bullets. According to Ras, a Nottingham teen:

❝ You can buy a bora for £10. If there are groups or gangs poaching customers, you are bound to get a turf war. If you are clocked [spotted] in a neighbourhood where you don't belong then you're gonna get capped [shot]. Everyone knows everyone in your hood, so new faces stick out. Outsiders aren't welcome. ❞

"Joining a gang is dangerous. Violent conflict between gangs is common, and gang members are at least 60 times more likely to be killed than the rest of the population."
Office of Juvenile Justice and Delinquency Prevention, USA, 1998.

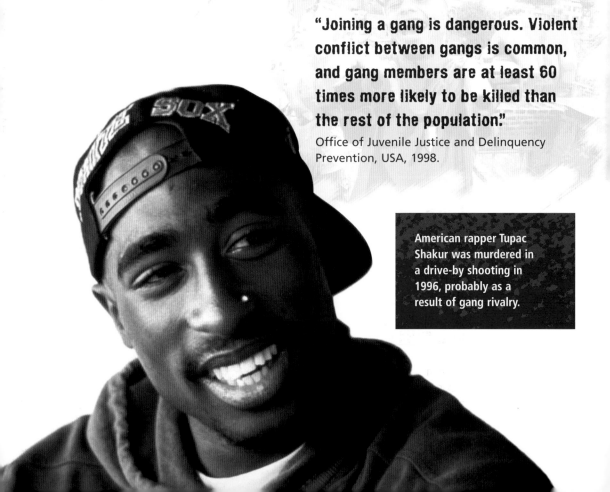

American rapper Tupac Shakur was murdered in a drive-by shooting in 1996, probably as a result of gang rivalry.

Drive-bys

One of the most violent means of attacking a rival gang is a drive-by shooting. Like most gang violence it can go wrong, as G-Roc, a member of the Crips, remembers:

❝ I don't really like to do drive-bys, because innocent people might get hit, you know? My homeboy shot a baby in the head. He felt bad about it, you know, but he was like, 'That's what happens sometimes'. ❞

Accidents are not the only way non-gang victims are targeted. Gangs often perform jacking – thefts of cars and other possessions, using violence. They also threaten, assault or torture non-gang members for money, to intimidate them to join their gang or to stop them reporting a crime to police. Some attack just for kicks.

ARE GANG MEMBERS VICTIMS OR VILLAINS?

Many countries are bringing in tougher laws against gangs. Should we be punishing them as a threat to society or thinking of gang members as victims of poor neighbourhoods?

Tougher laws

Gangs cause violent crime and misery. Gleen Reid lost her son, Corey. He was shot in a gang attack in Birmingham, UK. She has since become a leading member of Mothers Against Guns, a campaign group to get guns off the streets:

" The gangs try to recruit people, and if you are not with them, you are against them. The police are aware of what is going on, but no one seems to get locked up. It [using a gun] should carry a minimum sentence of at least ten years. That would make these young people think about spending time in prison. It would mean fewer guns and fewer killings. "

Members of the Torarot gang from the Philippines. Most people want those who indulge in gang violence to be punished.

A poor family in Birmingham, UK. It is often argued that poverty drives some young people into joining gangs.

No power, no future

Many gang members believe they had little alternative but to join a gang. Iris Sapp-Grant is a former member of the New York gang, the Deceptinettes. She came from a poor, gang-ridden neighbourhood:

❝ It was acted out every day in front of me. You had crazy people all around. You've got idiots hanging on the corner, and drug dealers were the ones making the money. It just didn't seem that there was any legit way out of it. We just learned how to become a part of that environment. Being violent and in a gang made me feel good, high and powerful – visible when before I had felt invisible and powerless. ❞

SHOOTINGS AND GANGS

An estimated 60% of all shootings in Manchester, UK between 1997 and 2000 were gang-related. Of all the gang-related shootings:

Offender gang member	23%
Victim gang member	37%
Both gang members	40%

DOES JAILING GANG MEMBERS WORK?

Mexican gang members are escorted to a New York court in May 2005.

In many countries, more gang members are being sent to prison for longer periods. In lots of US states it is now a crime to force someone under the age of 18 to join a street gang. Does prison stop gangs?

A sharp shock

Charlie was a member of the all-girl Scare Dem gang in the Midlands, UK. Her first time in jail shocked her into changing her life:

" I went to prison last year for five months and it shook me up. I hated it. I can't even describe it, I'm traumatised about it now.... I'm so glad for my freedom and I know that I can't go back there. Being away from your family, [with] all the drug addicts inside the prison... I just thought I don't belong here.... I now think all this violence and bling, bling rubbish will kill you, it's evil. Now I have a big conscience. "

Toughening up

Franck was 18 when he was sent to prison in the Netherlands for a violent gang crime. Instead of reforming him, contact with hardened criminals has made him a tougher gang member:

❝ Jail was no big deal. I went in a pussy, a weakling in my mind and in the body. I didn't like it, even cried myself to sleep. But I met real gangbangers in there. They taught me tricks, showed me how to be strong. I bulked up, I came out of jail as a man. Now, I'm back out on the streets, I've got major respect and I've gained serious juice [rank and status] in my gang. ❞

The inmates of the Ilopango women's prison in El Salvador are all Mara 18 gang members.

"They come back [from prison] much more schooled, polished, more brutal gang members."

Police Chief Art Lopez, California, 2004.

CAN GANGS BE STOPPED?

Tough laws and policing are only part of the solution to gangs. Anti-drugs campaigns and greater education about the dangers of gangs in schools can also help. Is enough being done?

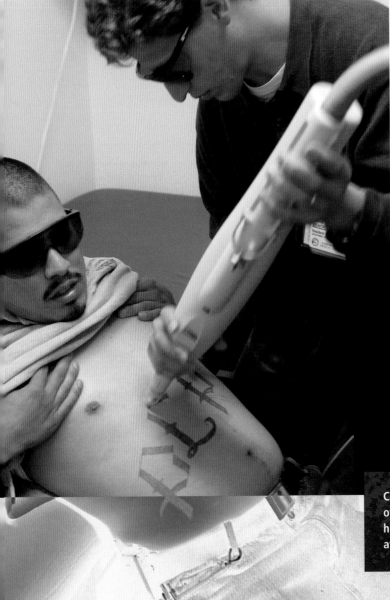

A safe haven

Most gangs form in tough, inner-city areas where there is little hope. Some schemes provide young people with safe and friendly places where they can hang out, away from gangs, and build their skills and interests. Dieter is a German teen who attends such a place in Dresden:

❝ At school and home, no one was interested in me, that's why I hung out in a gang. But at the centre, I get plenty of respect from the adults and the other kids. I play basketball and have been on rafting and adventure days. Rafting was great – I want to learn how to be an instructor. ❞

Carlos, a former member of the Players gang, gets his gang tattoos removed at a Los Angeles clinic.

Two members of a special gangs task force patrol the streets of Miami, Florida, USA.

No future

Gleen Reid of Mothers Against Guns in Birmingham (see p32) believes communities are not doing anywhere near enough to stop young people joining gangs:

❝ Young people have to be given something to look forward to. At the moment young people have got nothing, and they don't see much of a future. They are just living for today. We have to tell them to get armed with an education, not a gun. That way they can enjoy a prosperous life. We have got to help them, push them and be there for them.... It takes a couple to have a child, but it takes a community to raise a child. ❞

COMMUNITY POLICING

In Palermo, Italy, police officers went into the community to work with gangs and local residents directly, in order to try to reduce violence.

GANG-RELATED HOMICIDES	1995	1999	2000
	200	11	9

SHOULD PARENTS DO MORE TO HELP?

A rally organised by Mothers In Charge in Philadelphia, USA. Formed by mothers of murdered children, the group campaigns to reduce street violence.

Many gang members have troubled home lives and see the gang as their new family. Others come from happy family backgrounds. Are parents to blame for their sons and daughters joining gangs?

Stand up for yourself

Some people think it is not the parents' fault. Australian teenager, Asha, feels that it is up to the youths in gangs to take responsibility for what they do:

❝ Being in a gang means you are not strong enough to stand on your own, that if you get in a fight, you have to have your friends jump in with you to win, that you will betray your family and hurt people to get what you want. ❞

What can I do?

Some parents do their best but feel powerless in the face of gangs. Carl lives in Peckham, an area of south London, UK that has seen a massive rise in violent gang activity:

❝ I tell my sons that they have to go to school and study hard so they can make something of themselves, but they just laugh in my face. They say, 'Why should we study? So we end up like you? No thanks.' There are kids of 12 and 13 going out stealing every day, and they are making more money than their parents earn. How are you supposed to convince people like that you know what's best? Impossible. ❞

Members of El Salvador's National Academy of Public Safety clean up graffiti as part of the country's anti-gang plan.

"Teen gangs are lone children who turn to each other for support. Gang membership provides these young people with a sense of belonging that they do not benefit from anywhere else."
Camilla Batmanghelidjh, Director of Kids' Company, UK, 2004.

IS LEAVING A GANG EASY?

Getting out of a gang can be tough. Others in the gang may try to convince reluctant members to stay or threaten them or their families if they dare think of leaving.

Gang members may make the break safely, but others, like Squeaky of Inglewood, California, USA are terrified of what might happen to them:

66 My best friend Curtis was a member of the West Queen Street Gang. I made the mistake of asking if I could come along. There have been street fights and battles in the park. I have tried to leave the gang before but Curtis made it very clear – the only way I am leaving is in a box. 99

Many gang members are scared to leave because of fears of revenge, such as an arson attack on their home.

Jumping out

Some gangs may let a member leave after enduring a final fight or gang beating, called jumping out or beating out. Malice had to go through it to leave his New York gang:

This Gang 18 member in El Salvador is being beaten in to join. Beatings out can be even more severe.

❝ After three years in the gang I began to get tired of the lifestyle. I wanted to get out on my own so I could go to college or something, but I knew that I would have to take that last beating to get out. Luckily my homies understood and they put me up against a bunch of smaller guys in our set. I took my beating and was left with three bruised ribs, a fractured jaw and a dislocated shoulder. ❞

HOW TO GET OUT OF A GANG

When gang members decide they want to leave, there are a few steps they can follow:

● get help to develop a protection plan that can be followed

● begin spending time doing positive things

● make new friends

● stop looking like a gang member

● find people who will support them and believe in them

● be encouraged to believe in their own power to change.

From *Gang-Proof*, Public Safety Branch of Manitoba Justice, Canada, 2003.

CONCLUSION

Gangs remain a powerful option for some young people because they appear to offer things they feel they lack, such as power, support, money, protection and a sense of belonging.

Malice from Los Angeles feels that being in a gang helped him at a crucial time:

" Regardless of what anyone out there has to say, gangs saved my life. There was going to be violence anyway, regardless if I was involved in a gang or not. At least the Bloods gave me a sense of stability in my life. "

A scene from the 2004 film, *Redemption*, about the life of former gang member, Stanley 'Tookie' Williams.

Father Greg Boyle stands outside the Jobs for a Future centre in Los Angeles. The centre strives to offer members of the 60 or so East Los Angeles gangs a way out of gang life.

> "The advice I tell anyone who asks me that is quite simple: Don't join a gang. You won't find what you're looking for. All you will find is trouble, pain and sadness. I know. I did."
>
> Stanley 'Tookie' Williams, 2004.

Get out while you can

Others know that gang life nearly destroyed them and it was vital to get out. Scott was a member of the Crips:

> " I am an ex-Crip who has been out of the game since 1997. Was it easy? No! But it was something I needed to do not only for myself but my family. All I want to say is it can be done. For all of you who are thinking about getting out of gangs, do it before it's too late. "

Saying no

Saying no to joining a gang in the first place is an easier option than leaving a gang or living and possibly dying as a gang member. Stanley 'Tookie' Williams, a founder of the Crips in Los Angeles, was imprisoned for murder in 1981 Although he turned against gang violence, he was executed in December 2005.

TIMELINE

1600s Large numbers of street gangs appear in London, UK, including the Mims, the Hectors and the Dead Boys.

1790s New York and Philadelphia's first street gangs emerge.

1825 The Forty Thieves, the first American gang with a definite leadership, forms in New York.

1890s Notorious gangs such as the Five Points Gang form in New York.

1920s Studies show there are 1,313 gangs in Chicago with more than 25,000 members.

1936 Frederic M. Thrasher's book, *The Gang*, is published, one of the first scientific studies of gang ways and life.

1940s The Latin Kings gang for Hispanic gang members forms in Chicago.

1948 The famous motorcycle gang, the Hell's Angels, is formed.

1971 Stanley 'Tookie' Williams and Raymond Washington form the Crips in Los Angeles, which goes on to become one of the world's most infamous gangs.

1970s Vietnamese street gangs emerge in some of the USA's largest cities.

1981 Stanley 'Tookie' Williams is sentenced to the death penalty for murder.

1980s Crips gangs form in Central American countries such as Belize.

1980s Crack cocaine sweeps through the USA.

1980s The Tiny Rascals gang is formed by Cambodian immigrants in California. Within ten years it becomes the biggest Asian street gang in the USA.

1984 A 14-year-old girl and six bikers are killed in a gun battle between rival gangs in a suburb of Sydney, Australia.

1989 Immigrants from Belize form the Harlem Mafia Crips gang in New York, USA.

1993 Gang members in prison in one US state alone, Illinois (the state where Chicago is found), reach record levels of 17,489.

1996 Well-known rapper Tupac Shakur is killed in a drive-by shooting in Las Vegas, Nevada, USA.

1997 Gangster Disciples leader, Larry Hoover, and six other gang members, are convicted and sentenced to life imprisonment.

1997 Rapper Christopher Wallace, aka Notorious B.I.G., is shot to death in Los Angeles, USA.

2000 The alleged leader of the Latin Kings, Gustavo 'Gino' Colon, is sentenced to life imprisonment in Chicago, USA.

2001 Major gang battles take place outside Paris, France.

2003 An anti-gang law is passed in Central American country Honduras. Gang leaders face 9 to 12 years in prison, and many flee to Mexico or the USA.

2004 Suspected gang members massacre 28 bus passengers in the city of Chamalecon in northern Honduras.

2004 A 19-year-old gang member in Fort Worth, Texas, USA is sentenced to 30 years in prison for fatally shooting a childhood friend who wanted to leave their local street gang.

2005 US law enforcement officials across the country arrest 103 suspected members of the violent Mara Salvatrucha gang (also known as MS-13).

2005 Four members of the Burger Bar gang in Birmingham, UK are convicted of the murder of Charlene Ellis, aged 18, and Letisha Shakespeare, 17, in 2003.

2005 After more than 20 years on death row, Stanley 'Tookie' Williams is executed by Lethal inject.

GLOSSARY

addicts People who use drugs such as alcohol, cocaine or heroin and feel ill if they do not use them regularly.

beaten in Also 'jumped in': an initiation to become a member of a gang by being beaten by other gang members.

broken home A home in which the parents are divorced or one or both have left.

capped Shot.

dealers People selling illegal drugs, usually on the streets.

drive-by An attack, usually on a rival gang member, from a moving car and usually using guns.

endangerment To put oneself or someone else in danger or potential danger.

flashing Also sometimes called throwing signs: the symbols and shapes gang members make with their hands as a coded way of communicating with each other.

gangbanging To perform gang actions such as fighting and committing crime.

harass To annoy or upset someone over a period of time.

hardcore The most experienced and powerful members of a gang.

Hispanic Connected with Spain or Spanish-speaking countries such as the countries in Central and South America.

homies Short for home boys or home girls, it means a close friend, someone from the neighbourhood or a member of the same gang.

hood Short for neighbourhood.

intimidate To threaten or scare someone.

jacking Stealing using violence.

malnourished Weak and suffering from bad health because of a lack of food or a lack of healthy food.

narcotics Illegal drugs.

OGs Short for original gangsters, often veteran gang members or leaders.

role model A person whom someone admires and whose behaviour they try to copy.

tagger A person who puts up graffiti.

vandalism To damage or destroy others' property.

vulnerable Someone especially at risk.

wannabes Individuals who want to be gang members.

RESOURCES

Books

Crews: Gang Members Talk To Maria Hinojosa
by Maria Hinojosa and German Perez (Harcourt
Brace & Co., 1995)
Accounts from the streets from gang members
who answer questions put by a National Public
Radio reporter in the United States.

Gangs by Lisa Wolf (Lucent Books, 2000)
A serious and detailed study of gangs and
gang behaviour written for young teens.

Gangs & Bullies by Rosemary Stones (Evans,
1999)
A book complete with short case studies on
two issues affecting many young people today.

Gangs: Opposing Viewpoints by Laura K.
Egendorf, ed. (Greenhaven Press, 2001)
For older teen readers, an in-depth study of
the issues of gangs from different viewpoints.

Gangs (Looking at) by Julie Johnson
(Hodder Wayland, 2009)
A clear and simple look at gangs and how
people become members.

Websites

http://www.gangsorus.com
The website of gangs investigator Robert
Walker is packed with information and links
to other sites.

http://www.iir.com/nygc/faq.htm
A list of answers to Frequently Asked Questions
from the National Youth Gang Center.

http://www.nagia.org/
Website for National Alliance of Gang
Investigators Association. Includes a list of
useful websites.

http://www.streetgangs.com/
An in-depth look at the gangs in and around
Los Angeles, their history and the latest news.

INDEX

Numbers in *italics* refer to captions to illustrations

anti-gang campaigns 36
arson *40*
Australia 7, 24, 38, 44

Bamber, Katherine 7
beating in 10, 11, *11*, *41*, 46
beating out 41
Bloods gang *15*, 18, *24*, 42
bullying 7, 14

Canada 5, 29
capping 19, 30, 46
Central America 5, 27, *29*, *35*, *39*
children *5*, 6, *38*, 39
clothing 4, 18–19
Colombia *4*, 25
Colors 15
community policing 37
crime 4, 7, *10*, 12, 16, 23, *23*, 28
Crips gang *15*, *18*, 19, 31, 43, 44

Deceptinettes gang 33
drive-by shootings *30*, 31, 45, 46
drugs 15, 16, *23*, 26–27, *27*, 30, 33, 34, 36, 46

education 26, 36, 37

families 8, 38, 39
flashing *16*, 18, 19, 46
Flushing's Top Society gang 12
France 28

Gang 18 *16*
Gangster Disciples gang 22, 45
Germany *20*, 22, 36
girl gangs 7, 16–17, 34, *35*
graffiti 20–21, *20*, *21*, 23, 27, *39*, 46
guns *18*, 25, 32

history of gangs 8–9

identity 18–19
immigrants *22*, 44
initiation 11, 46

jacking 31, 46
joining gangs 10–11, 14–15, 43

leaving gangs 40–41, 43

Mafia Insane Vice Lords gang 15
Manitoba Warriors gang 11
Maoris 19
Mara 18 *13*, *29*, *35*
Mara Salvatrucha gang (MS-13) *11*, 18, 27, 45
maras 5
Mohawks gang 9
Mothers Against Guns 32, 37
Mothers in Charge *38*
murders 13, 16, 21, 28, 30, 32, 37

Nasty Fly Ladies gang 17
New Zealand 5, *19*

parents 38, 39
Pomona 12th Street gang 8
poverty *33*
prison 32, 34–35, 43

rap music 24
Redemption 42, 45
Rolling 20's Bloods gang *31*
Romeo and Juliet 8
Russia 4, *23*, 25

Scare Dem gang 34
school gangs 6–7
Shakur, Tupac *30*, 45
shootings 5, 19, 30, 33
  drive-by *30*, 31, 45, 46
shoplifting 7, *10*
Short Crew gang *5*
shottas 26
Sioux gang *22*

skinheads 4, *14*
South Africa *5*
stealing 7, 10, 25, 31, 39
symbols 18, 19, 20

ta moko 19
taggers 20, *21*, 46
tattoos 13, 18, *19*, *36*
Torarot gang *32*
turf wars 28, 30

UK 6, 10, 23, 32, *33*, 37, 39
  drug dealing 26
  gang history 9, 45
  gang numbers 5
  parents 32, 37
  prison 34
  shootings 32, 33
  turf wars 30

USA
  family gangs 8
  gang numbers 5
  getting out 40, 41, *43*
  girl gangs *17*, 33
  history 8, *9*, 44–45
  Los Angeles gangs *12*, 13, *18*, 19, 42
  murders 13, 28
  New York gangs 11, 12, 33
  parents *38*
  protection 22
  street gangs 4
  tattoos *36*
  youth gangs *9*

vandalism 20, 46
violence 4, 7, 12, 13, 16–17, 28–29, 30–31, *32*, 42
  drive-by shootings *30*, 31, 45, 46
  school gangs 7
  turf wars 30

weapons 16, *17*
  see also guns
West Queen Street Gang 40
Williams, Stanley 'Tookie' *42*, 43, 44, 45